NURSERY RHYMES

Mother Goose

# MOTHER GOOSE RHYMES

# Forecasting Fun

## WEATHER NURSERY RHYMES

compiled by Terry Pierce ❧ illustrated by Paula Knight

**PICTURE WINDOW BOOKS**
Minneapolis, Minnesota

Special thanks to our advisers for their expertise:

Terry Flaherty, Ph.D., Professor of English
Minnesota State University, Mankato

Susan Kesselring, M.A., Literacy Educator
Rosemount–Apple Valley–Eagan (Minnesota) School District

Editors: Christianne Jones and Dodie Marie Miller
Designer: Tracy Davies
Page Production: Angela Kilmer
Art Director: Nathan Gassman
The illustrations in this book were created digitally.

Editor's Note: Editorial and formatting decisions for most of the nursery rhymes in this book were based on the following source: *The Random House Book of Mother Goose* (1986), selected and illustrated by Arnold Lobel.

Picture Window Books
5115 Excelsior Boulevard
Suite 232
Minneapolis, MN 55416
877-845-8392
www.picturewindowbooks.com

**Library of Congress Cataloging-in-Publication Data**
Pierce, Terry.
Forecasting fun : weather nursery rhymes / compiled by Terry Pierce ; illustrated by Paula Knight.
p. cm. – (Mother Goose rhymes)
Summary: An illustrated collection of twenty nursery rhymes related to weather and the changing seasons.
ISBN-13: 978-1-4048-2347-1 (library binding)
ISBN-10: 1-4048-2347-6 (library binding)
ISBN-13: 978-1-4048-2353-2 (paperback)
ISBN-10: 1-4048-2353-0 (paperback)
1. Nursery rhymes. 2. Weather–Juvenile poetry.
3. Children's poetry. [1. Nursery rhymes. 2. Weather–Poetry.] I. Knight, Paula, ill. II. Mother Goose. Selections. III. Title. IV. Title: Weather nursery rhymes.
PZ8.3.P558643For 2006
398.8 E–dc22                    2006027246

# TABLE OF CONTENTS

# MOTHER GOO

# NURSERY RHYMES ABOUT WEATHER

**Do you like to SWIM in the SUMMER and SLED in the WINTER?** The four seasons bring special weather and special things to do. There are many nursery rhymes about the seasons and the weather. Can you find a rhyme about your favorite season or favorite type of weather?

# IT'S RAINING, IT'S POURING

It's raining, it's pouring,

The old man is snoring;

He got into bed

And bumped his head

And couldn't get up in the morning.

# ITSY BITSY SPIDER

The Itsy Bitsy Spider went up the water spout,

Down came the rain and washed the spider out.

Out came the sun and dried up all the rain;

And the Itsy Bitsy Spider climbed up the spout again.

# THE MONTHS

January brings the snow,
Makes our feet and fingers glow.

February brings the rain,
Thaws the frozen lake again.

March brings breezes sharp and chill,
Shakes the dancing daffodil.

April brings the primrose sweet,
Scatters daisies at our feet.

JANUARY

FEBRUARY

MARCH

APRIL

MAY

JUNE

**JULY**

**AUGUST**

**SEPTEMBER**

**OCTOBER**

**NOVEMBER**

**DECEMBER**

May brings flocks of pretty lambs,
Sporting round their fleecy dams.

June brings tulips, lilies, roses,
Fills the children's hands with posies.

Hot July brings thunder-showers,
Apricots, and gilly-flowers.

August brings the sheaves of corn;
Then the harvest home is borne.

Warm September brings the fruit;
Sportsmen then begin to shoot.

Brown October brings the pheasant,
Then to gather nuts is pleasant.

Dull November brings the blast—
Hark! the leaves are whirling fast.

Cold December brings the sleep,
Blazing fire, and Christmas treat.

# RAIN

Rain, rain, go away,
Come again another day,
Little Johnny wants to play.
Rain, rain, go to Spain.
Never show your face again.

# THIRTY DAYS HATH SEPTEMBER

Thirty days hath September,
April, June, and November;
All the rest have thirty-one,
Excepting February alone,
And that has twenty-eight days clear
And twenty-nine in each leap year.

# A RED SKY AT NIGHT

A red sky at night is a shepherd's delight;

A red sky in the morning is a shepherd's warning.

# MY LEARNED FRIEND AND NEIGHBOR PIG

My learned friend and neighbor pig,
Odds bobs and bills, and dash my wig!
It's said that you the weather know;
Please tell me when the wind will blow.

# THE WIND

When the wind is in the east,
'Tis neither good for man nor beast;

When the wind is in the north,
The skillful fisher goes not forth;

When the wind is in the south,
It blows the bait in the fishes' mouth;

When the wind is in the west,
Then 'tis at the very best.

15

# WHEN CLOUDS APPEAR

When clouds appear like rocks and towers,
The earth's refreshed by frequent showers.

# WHEN THE WIND BLOWS

When the wind blows,
Then the mill goes,
And our hearts
Are light and merry.

# ONE MISTY, MOISTY MORNING

One misty, moisty morning,
When cloudy was the weather,

I chanced to meet an old man
Clothed all in leather.

He began to compliment,
And I began to grin,

How do you do, and how do you do,
And how do you do again?

# THE SEASONS

Spring is showery, flowery, bowery;
Summer: hoppy, croppy, poppy;
Autumn: wheezy, sneezy, freezy;
Winter: slippy, drippy, nippy.

# APRIL WEATHER

April weather:

Rain and sunshine, both together.

# BLOW, WIND, BLOW!

Blow, wind, blow! and go, mill, go!

That the miller may grind his corn;

That the baker may take it,

And into bread make it,

And send us some hot in the morn.

# CALM WEATHER IN JUNE

Calm weather in June
Sets corn in tune.

# SIGNS OF THE SEASONS

A winter sled

A book read

An April shower

A spring flower

A summer day

A lad at play

Autumn; then

'Tis winter again.

24

# IT'S RAINING, IT'S RAINING

It's raining, it's raining,
There's pepper in the box,
And all the little ladies
Are holding up their frocks.

26

# WHEN THE PEACOCK
## ∼⊙ LOUDLY CALLS ⊙∼

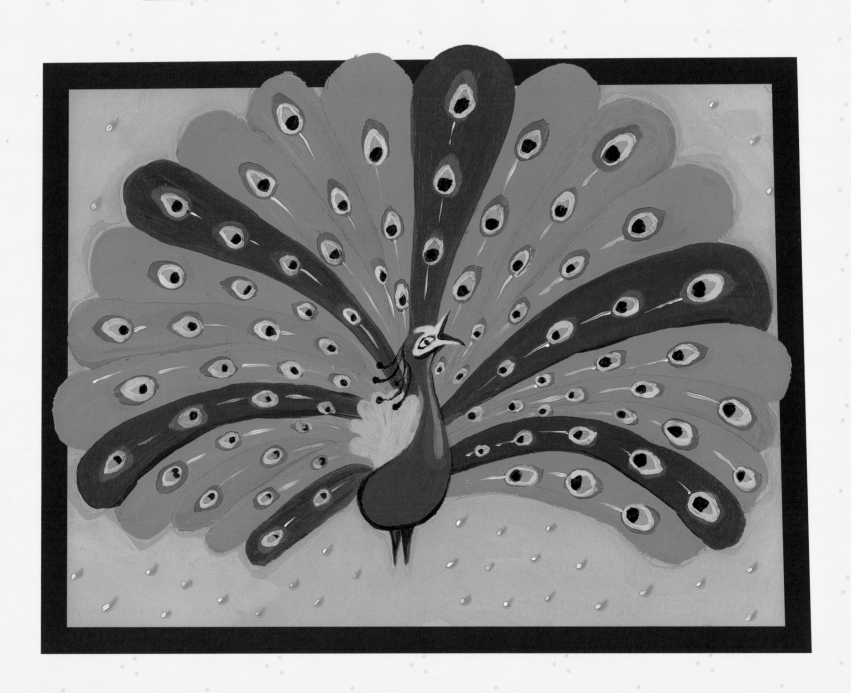

When the peacock loudly calls,
Then look out for rain and squalls.

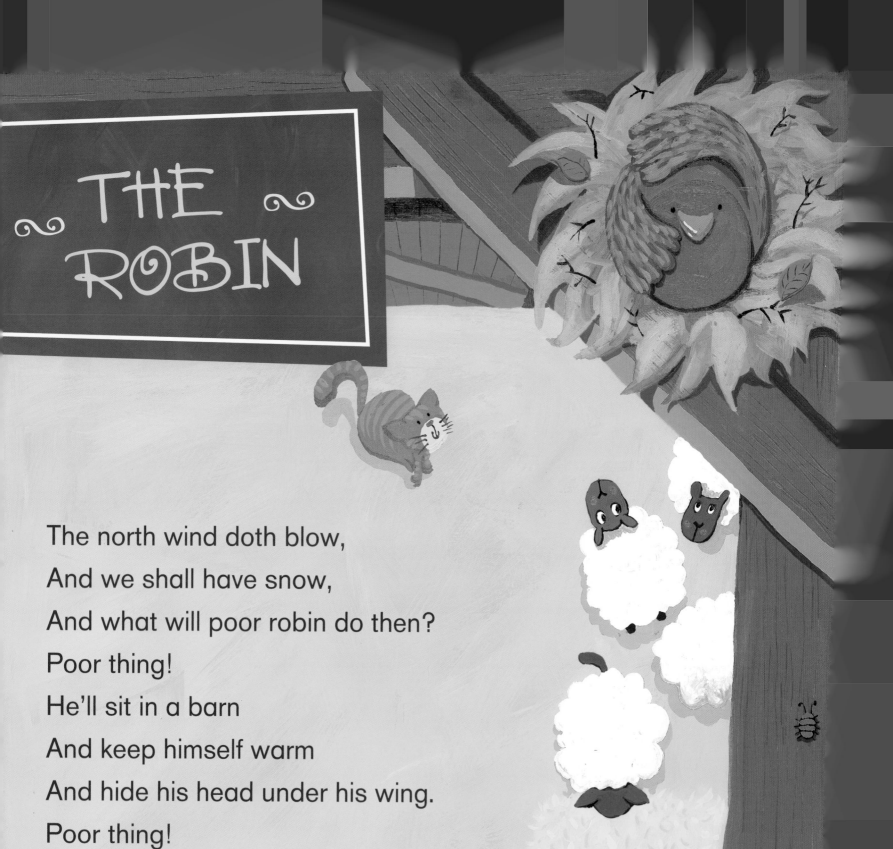

# THE ROBIN

The north wind doth blow,
And we shall have snow,
And what will poor robin do then?
Poor thing!
He'll sit in a barn
And keep himself warm
And hide his head under his wing.
Poor thing!

# ~ WINTER'S THUNDER ~

Winter's thunder
Is the world's wonder.

# THE HISTORY OF NURSERY RHYMES AND
# MOTHER GOOSE

∾

Nursery rhymes circulated orally for hundreds of years. In the 18th century, collectors wrote down the rhymes, printed them, and sold them to parents and other adults to help them remember the rhymes so they could share them with children.

Some of these collections were called "Mother Goose" collections. Nobody knows exactly who Mother Goose was (though there are plenty of myths about her), but she was probably a respected storyteller. Occasionally the rhymes commented on real people and events. The meaning of many of the rhymes has been lost, but the catchy rhythms remain.

Mother Goose nursery rhymes have evolved from many sources through time. From the 1600s until now, the appealing rhythms, rhymes, humor, and playfulness found in these verses, stories, and concepts contribute to what readers now know as Mother Goose nursery rhymes.

∾

# TO LEARN MORE

## AT THE LIBRARY

Delcher, Eden A. *Favorite Rhymes*. Baltimore: Allan
    Publishers, 1992.
Denton, Kady MacDonald. *A Child's Treasury of
    Nursery Rhymes*. New York: Kingfisher, 1998.
Eagle, Kin. *It's Raining, It's Pouring*. Milwaukee:
    G. Stevens Pub., 1996.

## ON THE WEB

FactHound offers a safe, fun way to find Web sites
related to this book. All of the sites on FactHound
have been researched by our staff.

1. Visit *www.facthound.com*
2. Type in this special code:
   1404823476
3. Click on the FETCH IT button.

Your trusty FactHound will fetch the best sites for you!

# INDEX OF FIRST LINES

## ☙ LOOK FOR ALL OF THE BOOKS IN THE ❧ MOTHER GOOSE RHYMES SERIES:

**Counting Your Way:** Number Nursery Rhymes
**Cuddly Critters:** Animal Nursery Rhymes
**Forecasting Fun:** Weather Nursery Rhymes
**Friendly Faces:** People Nursery Rhymes
**Sleepytime:** Bedtime Nursery Rhymes
**Ticktock:** Time Nursery Rhymes

Mother Goose

NURSERY RHYMES